PET
Science

PET SCIENCE

50 Purr-fectly Woof-Worthy Activities for You & Your Pets

Veronika Alice Gunter
& Rain Newcomb

Illustrated by
Tom LaBaff

LARK
BOOKS
A Division of Sterling Publishing Co., Inc.
New York

Creative Director,
Book and Cover Design
CELIA NARANJO

Illustrator
TOM LABAFF

Cover Illustration
TOM LABAFF

Art Assistant
BRADLEY NORRIS

Editorial Intern
SUE STIGLEMAN

Consultant
DR. RACHEL NORRIS

Library of Congress Cataloging-in-Publication Data

Gunter, Veronika Alice.
   Pet science : purr-fectly woof-worthy activities for you & your pets / by
Veronika Alice Gunter and Rain Newcomb ; illustrated by Tom LaBaff.— 1st ed.
      p. cm.
   Includes index.
   ISBN 1-57990-786-5 (hardcover)
   1. Pets—Miscellanea—Juvenile literature. 2. Dogs—Miscellanea—Juvenile literature.
   3. Cats—Miscellanea—Juvenile literature. 4. Science—Experiments—Juvenile literature.
I. Newcomb, Rain. II. LaBaff, Tom. III. Title.
SF416.2G86 2006
636.088'7—dc22

                                    2005024860

10 9 8 7 6 5 4 3 2 1

First Edition

Published by Lark Books, A Division of
Sterling Publishing Co., Inc.
387 Park Avenue South, New York, N.Y. 10016

Text © 2006, Lark Books
Illustrations © 2006, Tom LaBaff

Distributed in Canada by Sterling Publishing,
c/o Canadian Manda Group, 165 Dufferin Street
Toronto, Ontario, Canada M6K 3H6

Distributed in the United Kingdom by GMC Distribution Services,
Castle Place, 166 High Street, Lewes, East Sussex, England BN7 1XU

Distributed in Australia by Capricorn Link (Australia) Pty Ltd.,
P.O. Box 704, Windsor, NSW 2756 Australia

If you have questions or comments about this book, please contact:
Lark Books
67 Broadway
Asheville, NC 28801
(828) 253-0467

Manufactured in China

ISBN 13: 978-1-57990-786-0
ISBN 10: 1-57990-786-5

For information about custom editions, special sales, premium and corporate pur-
chases, please contact Sterling Special Sales Department at 800-805-5489 or
specialsales@sterlingpub.com.

To Lex Luthor, the greatest friend a family could have.

—*Tom LaBaff*

Contents

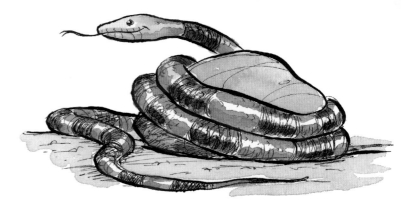

Pet-ology

Why do dogs drink out of toilet bowls? How do they instantly locate the leftover lunch buried deep in your book bag? How do parrots learn to talk? Why do cats get so perturbed when you blow on them, and what makes them purr? How can you tell when your fish is sleeping? Why do gerbils burrow?

Pet-loving, curious people like you have asked these questions for years. Now, three friends, Jessie, Lucinda, and Tim, have turned their prodigious brains to figuring out scientific answers to these puzzling questions. With the help of their animal friends, they designed experiments, tested theories, collected data, and figured out why pets do the things they do. You'll find 50 activities in this book that explore chemistry, biology, behavioral science, and more. They've named this new branch of science pet-ology.

A veterinarian helped Jessie, Lucinda, and Tim make sure that the projects are as much fun for your pets as they are for you. That's why you'll see Horatio, the vet's pet hermit

crab, whenever the vet has special tips about the activity. There are even some activities that your pets will love so much, they'll beg you to do them again and again. Best of all, this book will help you appreciate the unique personality of each of your pets, communicate better with them, and figure out what makes them happy.

If you want to see if your dog glows in the dark, learn to speak guinea pig, find out why snakes stick our their tongues, and figure out why your cat stalks your dirty socks, keep reading. This book is great even if you don't have pets (see page 12).

There are also tips for taking care of your pets and fascinating facts about all kinds of animals.

How to Use This Book

The first thing you need to do—even before you corral your cat or grab your gerbil—is to read all of the instructions for the activity you want to do. Don't skip this step. For each activity, you'll find the following elements:

What You Need lists all the materials and supplies you'll use in the activity. Gather everything you need before you get started. If you see the word "optional" after a supply, that means you don't have to use it to do the activity. Having it will usually just allow you more ways to experiment.

What You Do tells you how to perform the activity. Read through all the instructions and make sure you understand them before you begin.

What's Going On? explains the science behind the experiments. The fantastic answers come from brilliant people who work with animals and research why animals do the things they do.

When you see the words **"Pet Smarts,"** you've found health and safety tips. (Look for the hermit crab. He'll be hanging around, so you won't miss this important information.) These tips will help keep you and your pets safe. The **"Aha!"** boxes reveal surprising facts about animals. For instance, you'll read that guinea pigs aren't pigs (see page 21) and why fish float (see page 52). You'll also see in-depth reports about cat eyes, rat history, and more scattered throughout this book.

There's a glossary to help you with many of the science and pet terms. The words you see in bold-faced type (like **this**) are defined on pages 76 to 80.

How Not to Do the Activities

These activities are supposed to be FUN for you and your animal friends. If at any point your pet doesn't want to do it anymore, stop. If your pet would rather play or relax with you, do that instead. And if your pet wants a little time alone, let her have some peace and quiet.

Warning Signals

Watch your animal's body language. If she displays any one of these signals, stop the activity immediately.

Dogs

✔ Flattening her ears
✔ Tail between her legs
✔ Tail held stiffly straight up, possibly waving slowly back and forth
✔ Raised hackles
✔ Snarling
✔ Growling

Cats

✔ Twitching his tail jerkily
✔ Flattening his ears
✔ Snarling
✔ Hissing
✔ Bristled fur
✔ Spitting

If You Don't Have Pets

Sharing your home with a pet requires a lot of responsibility. A pet relies on you every single day for food, water, shelter, love, exercise, entertainment—everything!

But you don't need a pet to love animals—or to learn about them. Do the activities with a friend and his pet, with his parents' permission. Show this book to your teacher and ask to do activities with your class pet. Go to a nature center or zoo and do the **observation** activities, especially for **reptiles, birds**, and **felines**.

While you're there, ask if there are programs for volunteers to work directly with the animals that interest you the most.

There are more ways to be near animals without keeping them as pets. You can go on a school field trip to clean up polluted streams. That's a great way to see tadpoles and other fascinating **amphibians.** Find and join an environmental organization in your community that hosts forest clean-up days or nature hikes. Most have activities planned weekly or monthly, so you'll have lots of opportunities to go to new places. You might even see animals you never noticed before living right around the corner from you. Going on a safari to an exotic place is another way to see wild animals in their natural environment. If you prefer cuddly pets, you can volunteer for your local **humane society** at an **animal shelter** and find some new best friends. You can even bring a few of them home to stay—if you have permission, of course.

After Reading this Book....

Who are the scientists who discover fascinating things about animals? Which of these types of science sound most interesting to you?

Ethologists spend months in the wild observing—you guessed it—wild animals. They figure out how animals behave in their **natural environment.** You'll find lots of activities in this book that make the connection between your pet and his wild cousins.

Animal behaviorists work hard to find out what makes the **domesticated** version of those animals—your pets—do the things they do in their natural environment (your house!). That's part of the science behind the way your dog talks, the way your cat hunts, and more.

Even **biologists** and **zoologists** get in on the action, studying how animals' bodies work and how they adapt and survive in their environments. Then there are **veterinarians.** Vets are animal doctors, so they need to know how and why animals act and function the way they do so they can keep animals healthy and happy. Vets rely on the research of biologists and zoologists, plus their own studies and experiences.

Hide & Seek

Challenge your dog to find her favorite treats and toys.

What You Need

- Your dog
- Her treats or toys
- Empty boxes, couch cushions, and blankets

What You Do

1. Escort your dog from the room, so she won't see you hiding her stuff.

2. Hide her treats in the empty boxes, under the couch cushions, in a pile of blankets on the floor, and anywhere else you can think of. Make sure they're places your dog will be able to get into without causing any damage.

3. Bring your dog back into the room. Observe her. Does she notice that you've hidden treats in the room? How can you tell? What does she do?

What's Going On?

A dog's sense of smell is much more highly developed than a person's. That's why police officers, search and rescue teams, and handicapped people use dogs to help with their jobs or everyday lives. There are millions of special odor-sniffing **cells** in each dog's nose. The cells transmit information to the dog's brain, which processes each smell and determines what to do. (Eat it? Leave it? Pee on it?) That's why dogs can always find the chew-bone they buried outdoors—and how your dog found her treats. If your dog found them easily, conduct this experiment again using smaller pieces of dog treats and new hiding spots.

The Sniff Test

Use scientific methods to discover your cat's favorite spices.

What You Need

- Pencil and paper
- Your cat
- Nutmeg, allspice, cinnamon, mint leaves, and catnip
- Clean hardwood or linoleum floor

What You Do

1. Using the paper and pencil, make a chart listing the spices and leave room to record your cat's reaction to each one. (Use the spices in the order listed above.)

2. Sprinkle one spice at a time on the clean floor.

3. Bring your cat to the spice and watch him investigate it. What does he do? After he seems "done" investigating that spice, clean it up. Then sprinkle a different spice about 10 inches away. Repeat until you've used all the spices.

4. Is there a particular spice that he prefers? How do you know? Are there ones that he avoids? Make notes in your chart.

What's Going On?

Did your cat go bonkers, or could he not care less? Some smells **trigger** strong reactions in cats. Catnip is a plant whose smell triggers certain behaviors in approximately 70 percent of cats. Kitties who like catnip roll and chew on the leaves, maybe kick back their legs in abandon, and even bat pieces around and then chase and pounce on them.

Why some cats react is a mystery, but scientists have discovered that catnip contains a chemical called **nepetalactone,** which seems to **mimic** a **hormone** produced in cats. The hormone stimulates areas of the brain that control pleasure and excitement, and so does the catnip. There may be other smells that trigger these reactions in cats. How did your cat respond to the other spices?

Glow-in-the-Dark

A hairbrush and a black light are all it takes to make your pet shine.

What You Need

- Your dog or cat
- Dark room
- Black light*
- Brush

*Find at a discount store

What You Do

1. Lure your dog into a dark room.

2. Turn on the black light. Shine it on her fur. Do you see anything unusual?

3. Turn off the black light, and brush your pet. Turn the black light back on. Now what do you see? Is your pet glowing?

What's Going On?

Congratulations! You are the proud owner of a radioactive pet! Just kidding. If your dog was glowing, that's because she has **dandruff.** Dandruff consists of flakes of dead skin **cells.** These cells contain **phosphors**. A black light bulb produces ultraviolet light, which triggers the release of visible light from phosphors. (Phosphors are also in fluorescent posters, as well as white clothes washed in laundry detergent made with phosphors.)

A little bit of dandruff is normal, in people and in pets. If it's excessive (dropping onto the floor or making your pet's bed look snowy), talk to your veterinarian. She can recommend a routine for brushing, bathing, and feeding that can take care of dandruff. Extra pet dander isn't just messy—it can also cause allergic reactions in people who are sensitive to pet dander.

Aha!

Have you heard of a **hypoallergenic** pet? That's one who doesn't produce much dander, making a good pet for a person who is usually allergic to cats and dogs. Poodles don't have as much dander as other dogs. They also don't **shed**—but that doesn't mean they're maintenance-free. Poodle owners have to take good care of poodle hair, devoting two to five hours to grooming every week. The hair doesn't fall out and it grows constantly, so it has to be cut, especially around the mouth, eyes, and rear-end. Poodles also need to be brushed regularly. Otherwise, their hair gets matted— just like your hair would if you didn't brush it. Some people **mat** their poodle's hair on purpose, twisting it into beautiful dreadlocks. Dogs with this funky hairstyle are called "corded poodles."

Heat Hunter

Discover one of your snake's special skills with this simple experiment.

What You Need

- A rock
- A sunny day
- Your snake
- Spare aquarium or box with air holes

What You Do

1. Heat the rock by placing it in the sun for an hour. You could place it on a windowsill.

2. Check the rock. If it's too hot to touch comfortably, it is too hot for this experiment. (A too hot rock will kill your snake.) If it's too hot, let it cool in the shade.

3. When the rock is ready, put your snake in another aquarium or a box with air holes. You'll only leave her there for a minute or two.

4. Hide the rock in your snake's cage. Try putting it out of sight.

5. Return the snake to her cage and watch what she does.

What's Going On?

Did your snake **stalk** the rock, or immediately curl around it as if it were a snuggly teddy bear? Either way, your snake should have noticed the rock quickly, even if it was hidden from sight. There are two reasons why.

Snakes have heat-sensing **organs** where their ears would be. That's right, snakes don't have ears—and they don't hear. Snakes don't hear a mouse scurrying nearby; instead, they sense the mouse's **body heat**. So, your snake might check out the rock in this experiment to see if it's **prey**.

Also, a snake's skin senses warm objects, and she is attracted to the warmth. That's because snakes are **cold-blooded** animals, meaning they don't produce body heat the way you do. Snakes rely on warmth from their **environment** for their bodies to function. That's why you'll sometimes find snakes sunbathing, especially during cold weather.

Pet Smarts

Hot rocks, hot sunlight, hot anything can kill a **reptile**. Your pet won't know he's being burned until it's too late, so you have to look out for him. Talk to a veterinarian about where to put your pet's cage to avoid excessive heat and light, and ask for other tips to keep your pet healthy and safe.

Red Fish, Blue Fish

Can your fish see colors?

What You Do

1. Tape the blue and red paper to opposite sides of the fish tank (near the surface of the water).

2. Drop food into the tank next to the red paper.

3. After your fish has eaten all the food, remove both pieces of paper.

4. Repeat this process every time you feed your fish for one week.

5. Switch the pieces of paper so they're taped to different sides of the tank. Can your fish figure out where the food will be?

What's Going On?

Did your fish learn to associate food with the color red? If so, that's because some fish have **color vision.** Vision is important for fish: it helps them find food, avoid **predators,** and seek shelter. Because a fish's eyes are located on the sides of his head, he can see in almost every direction without moving his head. Animals have eyelids to protect and moisten their eyes. But most fish don't have eyelids. They don't need them, because fish are always surrounded by water!

Try this experiment using different colors. Are there any colors your fish can't see?

FEED US!
FEED US!
FEED US!

Do You Speak Guinea Pig?

Listen to your guinea pig. He'll tell you what's going on.

What You Need

- Your guinea pig

What You Do

1. Listen to the various sounds your guinea pig makes throughout the day (and night).

2. See if you can match the sounds to those in the list on the next page.

> chatter chatter purr moan moan chatter coo coo coo purr purr squeak squeak purr purr squeak chatter coo coo chatter squeak squeak!

3. Compare the sounds to your guinea pig's behavior. What sounds does he make when he's angry? Happy? Hungry? How does he move his body when he makes the different noises?

Guinea Pig Vocabulary

Coo: I'm happy and everything is going well.

Purr: I love you (twitching hips and swaying body).

Loud purr: I feel aggressive (marching in place).

Teeth chatter: Stay away; you're making me mad (swaying side to side). Be careful when your pet makes this noise. It's one of the few occasions when your guinea pig might bite you.

Moan: Leave me alone, please. This is usually directed at another guinea pig who wants to play or cuddle.

Low-pitch squeak: I'm having a normal guinea pig conversation.

High-pitch squeak: I'm annoyed.

Continuous high-pitch squeak: I'm excited.

Very high-pitch squeak: I'm scared, hurt, or trying to warn others.

Brr: I'm puzzled by a new sound, smell, or person.

4. Use the information you've discovered to change how you and your family play with your guinea pig.

What's Going On?

Your guinea pig makes lots of different noises and uses specific sounds to **communicate** certain messages. (See the vocabulary chart.) That's because guinea pigs are **herd** animals. In the wild, they live in groups (usually one dominant male, several females, plus younger males) and use their voices and **body language** to talk. Guinea pigs have also been known to sing. They have a birdlike, chirping song. Other guinea pigs stop in their tracks and listen whenever they hear it. One theory is that the song was used as a warning call in the wild. Or maybe it's just guinea pig opera.

Aha!

Guinea pigs aren't related to pigs. They're **rodents**, originally from the Andes Mountains in Peru. The Incas, a group of people who created an empire in South America, **domesticated** guinea pigs and ate them. (Some people still use them for food.)

Seventeenth-century European explorers brought guinea pigs home with them. They liked them better as pets than as meals.

Paw Prints

Is your pet a hunter? A wanderer? A scampering thief?

What You Need

- Your pet
- Mud
- Scissors
- Empty cardboard milk or juice container
- Butter knife
- Petroleum jelly or vegetable oil
- Water
- Quick-dry plaster of Paris*
- Spoon
- Trowel
- Pie pan or cookie sheet

*Find at a discount store

What You Do

1. Convince your pet to walk through the mud, leaving paw prints.

2. With the scissors, cut the top off the empty cardboard container. Cut a strip 2 to 3 inches wide from the remaining part, making a small square enclosure for one paw print.

3. Using a butter knife, spread petroleum jelly on the inside of the square. Then carefully place the square over the paw print. The cardboard needs to keep the plaster from spreading out, so make sure there are no gaps between the square and the ground.

4. Add water to the plaster of Paris according to the instructions; stir with a spoon. (You can use the leftover part of the cardboard container.) It should look like pudding when you're done.

5. Pour the plaster into the paw print. The plaster should be about 1 inch deep. Let it set for 30 minutes.

6. With the trowel, dig around and beneath the paw print, keeping the cardboard in place. Transfer the whole heap (plaster, dirt, and all) onto a pie pan. Bring it inside and let it dry overnight.

7. Remove the cardboard from the cast, turn over the cast, and brush the dirt off the other side.

What's Going On?

Paw prints can tell us a great deal about an animal. The number of toes, for instance, tells us about **locomotion.** A horse has a single hoofed toe, specially adapted for fast running over hard ground. A parrot has several long toes for climbing on branches and holding food.

Paw prints also reveal types of **claws**. The sharp, thin claws of a cat are meant for grabbing and holding onto **prey**, as well as for climbing trees. The large, thick claws of a dog give her **traction** to run over all kinds of **terrain**, and also make her an excellent digger.

Paw prints show that many animals have **footpads**. Made of thick layers of skin, footpads provide cushioning on rough surfaces. (Like built-in sneakers!)

Paw prints also reveal foot size. Most animals have feet **proportional** to their bodies. But some animals need specially sized feet. Think of a rabbit or a kangaroo's large hind feet. These give him tremendous jumping power. (Since the front feet aren't used for jumping, they are proportional to the rest of the body, so they look just the right size.)

Sitting Pretty

Get ready to see some bird acrobatics when you offer your pet a new perch.

What You Need

- Your bird
- Your bird's cage
- The cage you move your bird to while you clean her cage
- Several tree branches of various diameters

What You Do

1. Move your bird out of her cage, to a safe place, such as another cage.

2. Place the branches in secure locations in her cage. Put some at weird angles. Make sure they can support her weight so she will not fall if she climbs them. If the cage is small, you may need to use just one branch at a time.

3. Move your bird into her cage and shut the cage door.

4. Watch your bird to see what she does with the branches. Does she have a favorite?

What's Going On?

Did your bird climb the branches? Did she go upside down and sideways, too? Birds are highly intelligent and entertain themselves by finding many ways to scale just about anything you put in their cages. Having a new surface to touch and climb is mentally and physically stimulating. It gives bird bodies and brains a workout. Tree branches make especially good **perches** for birds because they are irregular and have a natural texture. And birds **instinctually** like the feel of a tree.

Pet Smarts

Wanna give your bird some ladders and swings? Check with your vet first. Toys and accessories can be hazardous to your pet depending on the materials and design. For instance, some plastics and paints are toxic to birds.

Mirror, Mirror

Who is the fairest bird on the wall?

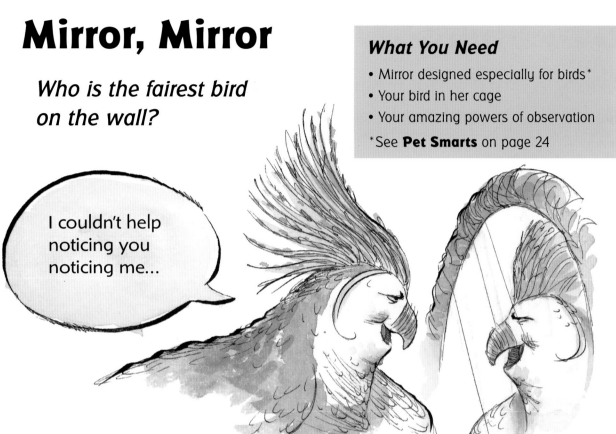

I couldn't help noticing you noticing me...

What You Do

1. Place the mirror inside your bird's cage, positioned so your bird can see herself. Shut her cage door.

2. Watch your bird approach the mirror. What does she do when she looks in the mirror? Is her behavior any different than usual?

What's Going On?

Most birds are very responsive to **visual images**. This means they pay attention to what they see, and what they see affects how they behave. This is a good **instinct** to have, since birds are hunted by **predators**, including snakes, cats, and other birds. If your bird looked in the mirror and saw herself, she may have done some interesting **postures** or **vocalizations**. Did she understand that she was looking at herself, or did she think it was another bird that might be her new companion? Based on what she did, what do you think? If you have your cat or dog look in a mirror, how do they react? Try a new experiment: one at a time, show your bird a magazine picture of a bird, a photograph of you, and a photograph of you hung upside-down. How does she react to each?

Dog Brains

Finally, a few tests to answer the ultimate question: How smart is your dog?

Short-Term Memory Test

What You Need

- Your dog
- Dog treats
- Stopwatch or watch with a second hand

What You Do

1. With your dog in the room, hide her treat somewhere. Let her watch you do it.

2. Take your dog out of the room. Wait 30 seconds.

3. Take your dog back into the room and start the stopwatch. Time how long it takes her to find the treat.

What's Going On?

You tested your dog's **short-term memory**. It's entirely likely that she did NOT find the treat quickly. Dogs seem to learn by **repetition**. Although your dog may not remember where the treat is the first time you do the experiment, if you hide a treat in the same spot every day for a week, she will likely check it frequently—even when you aren't playing together. The more often she is rewarded with a treat, the more likely she will repeat the behavior of looking in that hiding spot.

Long-Term Memory Test

What You Do

1. With your dog in the room, hide her treat somewhere. Let her watch you do it.

2. Take your dog out of the room. Wait 5 minutes.

3. Take your dog back into the room and start the stopwatch. Time how long it takes her to find the treat. If your dog does well, repeat steps 1 through 3 and increase the time you wait outside the room to 10 minutes.

4. If your dog is still enjoying this game, introduce some distractions. When you take her out of the room, play her favorite game for a while, or take her for a walk. Then see whether she remembers where the treat is.

What's Going On?

Did your dog get faster each time? For people and animals, a lesson is likely to be committed to **long-term memory** if it has been repeated several times. The brain creates special shortcuts for frequently used areas of the brain. So, when a lesson is repeated over and over, it becomes easier to remember because the brain no longer has to think about it. The brain just knows what's going to happen next. It's actually easier for a dog to learn a lesson than it is for a person, because people are capable of choosing not to learn.

Flashcard Feats

Test how quickly your rat can learn the symbol for food.

What You Need

- Marker
- 2 index cards
- Rat treats*

* When doing this kind of experiment, use TINY food treats. (You can break treats into very small pieces.) Otherwise, your rat may become full before you finish the experiment!

What You Do

1. With the marker, draw a triangle on one index card and a circle on the other.

2. Show the triangle index card to your rat. Immediately give her a treat. Repeat this at least five times. Do the same with the circle index card, but without giving her a treat. Repeat this at least five times.

3. Set both index cards in front of your rat. Does she show more interest in the triangle or the circle? If she touches the triangle card, give her a treat. If she touches it again, give her another treat, and so on

What's Going On?

Did your rat figure out that touching the triangle earned her a treat? Did she touch it so many times you ran out of treats? Rats are very intelligent and capable of learning complex activities. Rats learn by **repetition**, and are able to associate rewards (treats!) with sounds, shapes, colors, and activities. The more a **behavior** is rewarded, the more likely it is to be repeated. If the treats stop, the behavior will die out. Repeat this experiment with your rat a week later and see how quickly she chooses the triangle. If she gets really good at this, add one more card with a distinct shape (rectangle, star) each week and see how many cards she can sort through to find the triangle.

The Rat's Bad Rap

You've heard these expressions before: "You dirty rat." "It's a rat race out there." "Don't rat me out." "Rat fink!" or simply "Rats!" when something messes up. Comparing a person to a rat implies that he's selfish, untrustworthy, crude, and unattractive. People think that rats are unclean, vicious pests that steal food and spread disease. How did your cute, playful, intelligent, clean rat's family get such a bad reputation?

Okay, so **wild** rats did carry the bubonic plague to Europe in 1347. Over the course of five years, the disease infected and killed about 25 million people—approximately one-third of the human population at the time. But it also killed most of the rats. And the Oriental Flea was the actual disease-causing culprit. (People and animals bitten by the fleas developed the plague.) The rats died horrible plague-induced deaths too, but everybody forgets about that fact.

But the plague occurred almost 700 years ago. Seven hundred years ago, your human ancestors refused to bathe, believing that washing was an unhealthy practice. But nobody insists on calling *you* a stinker because of it!

So why do so many humans loathe rats? Maybe it's because rats travel in large numbers when frightened from their homes, appear fearless, and can get into and onto just about anything. People are afraid of being bitten by wild rats, too. Most reported bites happen to children, which understandably freaks out parents. Wild rat bites generally occur in overcrowded neighborhoods, near alleys, sewers, subways, garbage dumps, and zoos. Diseases transmitted by rat bites are rare. In fact, there's never been a documented case of rabies spread by rats in the United States.

Rats and other rodents are also held responsible for eating, spoiling, or destroying between one-fifth and one-third of the world's food supply for humans. Hey, everybody's got to eat! The fact is, wild rats are opportunists, so of course they'll dine wherever humans leave food (barns, kitchen pantries, alleys) and take refuge anywhere people provide warmth (homes, other buildings).

Favorite Foods

Which chow will your pet choose?

What You Need

- Your dog (or cat)
- Canned, small dry kibble, and large dry kibble types of the same brand and flavor of dog (or cat) food, about one serving of each
- Three clean identical bowls

What You Do

1. Make sure your dog has had something to eat within six hours, so she's not super-hungry. Put ¼ serving of each kind of dog food in each bowl.

2. Set the bowls next to each other. Note the order of the food types.

3. Bring your dog into the room. Watch her check out the foods. See which food she eats first.

4. Repeat steps 1 through 3 with the types of food in a different order than previously. (Otherwise, your dog might just be picking the same bowl.)

What's Going On?

Did your dog have an immediate preference for one type of food? Or did she try each kind and then eat her favorite? Using the same brand and flavor of food makes it more likely that your dog is picking the food based on its texture and size (instead of flavor—which she can smell). Any dog can have **sensitive** teeth and prefer soft food. Small dogs often prefer little chunks for their little mouths; large dogs tend to like large chunks. Did your dog eat all the food? Approximately 70 percent of pet dogs are **overweight**. They don't know when to stop eating, and will even try to eat food that's bad for them. (Like chocolate, which can be **toxic**.)

Pet Smarts

Do not perform this experiment if your dog is protective of her food or acts aggressive while eating. Make sure the food you use will not upset your dog's stomach. (If you have any questions, ask your veterinarian before performing this experiment.)

Aha!

Some dogs will eat **inedible** objects, such as socks, wood, and plastic. Usually they start chewing for fun or to sharpen their teeth, and pieces break off and they swallow them. Dogs can get sick or even die from chewing on the wrong things. For tips on safe **chew toys**, talk to your vet.

What's for Dinner?

What kind of food does your rabbit like?

What You Need

- Beef or turkey lunchmeat, carrots, broccoli, and kale
- Dish
- Your rabbit

What You Do

1. Put small amounts of each food in the dish.

2. Offer the dish to your rabbit.

3. What does he do? Which food does he prefer?

What's Going On?

Your rabbit won't touch the meat, but will eat every single bit of the vegetables. That's because rabbits are strict **herbivores,** which means they eat only plants. Their **digestive systems** are designed to extract **nutrients** from plants. To help do this, they have a large out-pouching of their **intestinal tract,** called a **cecum.** The cecum **ferments** grasses, hay, and vegetables into substances the rabbit's body can use.

Rabbits need to eat coarse foods, such as **hay,** to help grind down their constantly growing teeth. Vets sometimes recommend that pet rabbits have their front teeth trimmed regularly to prevent them from growing too large and damaging their mouth.

Pet Smarts

If your rabbit is not used to eating different types of vegetables, consult with your veterinarian before doing this experiment. The vet may suggest you feed your rabbit only a tiny amount, so his **digestive tract** can adjust to eating new foods. Too much new food can give him diarrhea, which can be very dangerous.

HAM

Roast Beef

Pet Fashion

Which skin covering is best for your pet?

What You Need

- Hair from your pet's brush *
- Fallen bird feathers *
- Snake scales
- Several empty toilet paper tubes
- Packing or duct tape
- Pencil and paper
- Digital thermometer

* Collect over several days, if necessary. Never cut your pet's fur or feathers without a veterinarian's advice.

What You Do

1. Collect the fur, feathers, and scales—whatever you can find.

2. Cover one end of each toilet paper tube with the tape so that the sticky side is facing the inside of the tube.

3. Stuff one type of material into each toilet paper tube, so that you have one with feathers, one with cat fur, one with dog fur, etc. Use the pencil to label each tube.

4. Set the tubes side by side on a flat surface, away from any heat source (sunlight, heat duct, etc.).

5. Check to make sure the digital thermometer is working. Write down the temperature on the paper. Then take turns sticking the thermometer into each tube and waiting five minutes. Each time you take the thermometer out, write down the new temperature on the paper.

What's Going On?

The temperature most likely remained **constant** (the same) in the fur and feathers tubes, but decreased in the scales tube. Why the differences? Because animal **skin coverings** provide different amounts of **insulation**, depending on how warm or cool the animal needs to be in his natural **environment**. Don't forget that feathers, fur, and scales don't naturally exist apart from the bodies they come from. The coverings can only keep a body warm if the body is warm to begin with. So it matters if the animal is **warm-blooded** (producing its own body heat) or **cold-blooded** (absorbing heat from the environment).

An animal's **metabolism** controls the body's ability to produce heat. To conserve heat, **warm-blooded** animals rely on **body fat** to keep them warm, and then the skin covering keeps the warmth in. Some squirrels, mice, and even human infants have a special type of fat called **brown fat**. Brown fat has the ability to generate heat. It helps animals survive in cold weather. Feathers make very good insulation, but birds in cold climates still have to eat large amounts of food to fuel their metabolisms and keep warm. Most creatures with scales are cold-blooded, so they don't need to insulate their bodies from hot or cold temperatures: they just become that temperature.

Aha!

Does your dog or cat **blow her coat**? That's what you call it when she suddenly **sheds** lots of hair over the course of a few days or a few weeks. An animal's hair is called a **coat**. Most animals have two coats: an outer coat and an undercoat. Generally, **warm-blooded animals** that inhabit colder **climates** have soft, long coats, and animals in warmer climates have bristly, short coats. It's perfectly normal for a dog or cat to blow her coat once or more a year. You can help her out by brushing her three times a week year-round. Most pets learn to love **grooming** time with you.

Four-footed Weather Forecasters

Can your pet tell you when a thunderstorm's approaching?

What You Need

- Weather forecast
- Your dog or cat
- Watch

What You Do

1. Find your local forecast. Identify the next day it's expected to thunder and do this experiment on that day.

2. Watch your pet. See if your pet exhibits any unusual behavior as the storm nears—before it thunders.

3. Use your watch to time how long it takes for the storm to arrive after your pet started acting funny.

What's Going On?

Did your pet prick up her ears, start pacing quickly, or whine to come inside before the thunderstorm? People have debated for a while about whether or not animals can predict the weather. Some people theorize that four-footed animals can sense rainstorms because of the thunder that accompanies them. Thunder creates vibrations that travel through the ground. Animals with their paws on the ground will sense the vibrations and know a storm is on its way. Some people think it's the animal's super-sensitive hearing that alerts them to the presence of an approaching storm. No one knows for sure if animals can predict the weather or not. Can yours?

E.S.P. (Extra-Smart Pet)

Does your dog have psychic powers?

What You Do

1. Set the clock and the watch to the same time. Give your helper the clock, paper, and pencil and ask him to watch your dog and record what she does and the time at which she does it. (He can use the chart on page 46.)

2. Leave the house and take the watch. Go somewhere for several hours. Don't tell your helper or your dog how long you'll be gone.

3. When you decide to go home, look at the watch. Make a note of what time it is and go home.

4. When you get home, look at your helper's notes to see whether your dog's behavior changed when you started heading home, when you walked up to the door, or when you walked in the door.

What's Going On?

Although there's no scientific evidence that dogs are **psychic** or have **extra-sensory perception**, they do occasionally seem to know when things are going to happen. It's possible that they use their senses (hearing, smell), which are much, much more perceptive than ours. For instance, if you rode a bike during the experiment, your dog may have noticed its unique spinning sound from $1/4$ mile away. Dogs, being **pack animals**, also watch what you do constantly. What you do (without realizing it) may trigger certain doggie behaviors that convince you that your dog is reading your mind. For instance, your dog notices the slightest change of expression on your face. So if you think about how much fun it would be to go for a walk and your face brightens a bit, don't be surprised if suddenly your dog is nudging your hand and offering to go out with you!

Cat Scratching

Experiment to find what your cat likes to stick his claws in — besides your couch.

What You Need

- Pencil and paper
- A scratching post made of carpet, or a scrap piece of carpet
- A scratching post made of sisal, or a scrap length of sisal
- A small board
- A piece of corrugated cardboard
- A piece of cereal box
- A piece of burlap
- Your cat

What You Do

1. With the pencil and paper, make a chart listing each item you collected, leaving room for you to write down how your cat responds to each one.

2. Set out all the objects from the list above in a room your cat spends lots of time in. Bring your cat into the room. You may need to pantomime scratching on the item, if necessary, and you may need to leave your cat alone with each item for a while before he'll play with it.

3. Watch what your cat does with each item. Does he scratch it up a little, ignore it, or attack it?

What's Going On?

Your cat probably found one or more items that he liked sinking his claws into. That's because scratching is an **instinct** that serves a lot of purposes. Scratching sharpens his **claws** so he's always ready to hunt or protect himself and his family. It's also a way for him to claim territory by leaving a visible mark, plus a scent called a **pheromone.** Marking territory is a habit cat ancestors developed to warn other cats to stay away from a family's living and hunting area. (**Glands** in cat paws secrete the pheromones. You can't smell them, but cats and dogs can.) Scratching also keeps your cat's feet healthy by stretching and conditioning the **tendons** in his toes, and exercises his leg and shoulder muscles.

Pet Smarts

Want to save your furniture from cat scratches? Make sure each cat in your household has his own place to scratch. Provide one to two **scratching posts** for each cat, tall enough for the cat to stretch to his full body length (about 3 feet for the average cat). Posts made from cardboard and burlap are the best choices, because your cat can leave his mark on them, to indicate to the other cats that it's his. And don't let your cats in the same room as the furniture that attracts their scratching. If you can't do that, instead place the posts near the problem furniture and rub some **catnip** on the posts.

Aha!

Why does your cat knead you with his claws before he sits down on your lap? Because he's claiming your lap as his special spot! Kneading releases **pheromones** from your cat's feet. The scent of these pheromones comforts him and leaves a mark to other cats that he was there *first*.

Kitty's Claws

A cat's **claws** are one of his most powerful weapons and handiest tools. His claws are razor-sharp and he keeps them sheathed inside his paw until he needs to use them. For this reason, they're called **retractable claws**. A tendon inside the cat's foot extends when he flexes the muscles in his foreleg, thrusting his claws out.

Cats use their claws for everything from **grooming** to self-defense, climbing, and exercise. That explains how your cat can go from gently brushing himself to taking a swipe at a dog who steps on his tail. Claws make it easy for cats to climb trees. He sinks his claws into the bark, and each claw acts as a hook. His weight keeps his claws sunk in. That's also why cats climb down trees backward. If he tries to go down the tree head first, his weight pushes his claws out of the bark. He can't get a grip! If a cat is scared, he might wait for someone to rescue him from the tree.

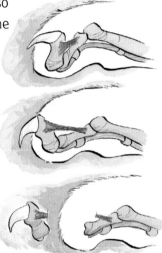

Cats keep their claws and bodies in good condition by scratching. Scratching **sheds** extra layers, sort of like you do when you trim your fingernails. The action also exercises cats feet, legs, and shoulders.

Some people can't stand that their cats like to climb and need to scratch, so they have their cats **declawed**. Declawing is a controversial surgery. In order to remove a cat's claws, his toe is **amputated**. On your hand, it would mean cutting off the tips of each of your fingers down to the first knuckle. A cat deprived of his claws can become distressed, out-of-shape, and anxious. For these reasons declawing is illegal in 24 countries, and some vets refuse to perform it.

If you're having problems with your cat, talk to your vet about training him to use his claws without getting in trouble.

Slither, Scamper, Hop

Experiment with locomotion:
try getting around the way your pets do.

Horsing Around

What You Do

1. Get down on all fours. Pretend that your hands are front paws and your feet are rear paws.

2. Move your right hand and your left foot at the same time; then move your left hand and your right foot, and so on. This is how horses, cats, and dogs move.

Slink and Slide

What You Do

1. Lie facedown on the floor with your arms close against your sides and your legs fairly straight.

2. Rock gently side-to-side while stretching your whole body forward, including your neck and head. Pause, then rock and stretch again. Don't push off with your hands, knees, chest, hips, or any other body part.

3. Repeat until you've moved yourself one body-length forward. How do snakes move so quickly?

Rabbit Running

What You Do

1. Get down on all fours. Pretend that your hands are front paws and your feet are rear paws.

2. Reach forward with both hands as far as you can, and then bring your feet in front of and to either side of your hands, and try to push off again with your feet. This is how rabbits, mice, and other rodents move.

What's Going On?

It's difficult and tiring to move like an animal, isn't it? Did you get far as a snake? You may have lost your balance trying the Rabbit Running. A lot of people do. That's because even though hopping is a great way for rabbits to move, you just aren't made to go that way.

People are **bipedal** (two legs), and many animals are **quadruped** (four legs). Every body is designed to help its owner go about the daily business of survival. Humans use their hands all the time and walk on their back "paws," leaving the front ones free to grab and hold things. Dogs keep all four legs on the ground. This makes them run faster, which helped them catch their **prey** when they were wolves, and keeps their head near the ground so that they can smell tracks and pick things up with their mouths. Rabbits have to be able to run away from fast preda-

tors, so their back legs are even stronger than a dog's, which allows them to move more quickly over short distances—and into the safety of a rabbit hole.

Some animals, including snakes, have no legs at all. But they make getting around look easy. A snake's body is full of muscles and a flexible **backbone** made up of up to 400 **vertebrae**. Snakes use full-body muscle power to move: they rock side-to-side while stretching and contracting their muscles. The result? They shoot forward. Some snakes move slightly to one side instead of directly forward, and some wind themselves in the shape of an S as they move.

Swim Olympics

Can the losers blame it on their swimsuits?

What You Need

- Pencil and paper
- Sketch pad (optional)
- Several different types of fish in an aquarium
- Ruler (optional)
- Your amazing powers of observation
- Stopwatch (optional)
- Masking tape

What You Do

1. With pencil and paper, make a chart that includes a sketch of each fish, each fish's name, and room to note how each one moves, and how fast.

2. Watch the fish swim in the tank. How does each one move around? (Does she flick her fins? Does he wiggle his tail?)

3. Which fish swim faster than others? (They don't have to be racing; just observe them at their normal pace.)

4. If you'd like, you can use the ruler and stopwatch to time how long it takes different fish to go the same distance. Mark off 10 inches with the ruler. Tape two pieces of masking tape to the tank to mark the start and finish lines. Use the stopwatch to time how long it takes each fish to go that distance.

What's Going On?

Have you noticed that running in a pool or in the ocean is more difficult than running on land? That's because water is heavier than air, so it takes more **energy** for your legs to **displace** water. A fish's body, however, is designed according to his individual needs—which is what you saw in this activity.

Some fish have streamlined bodies that reduce **drag** from the water and help them move faster to catch **prey**—or escape **predators**. (Think of a shark's long, lean body shooting forward to catch fish.) Other fish, such as the seahorse, swim upright by using small **dorsal** and **pectoral fins**. Seahorses aren't fast swimmers, but those fins enable them to wait for food to float their way. Another type of swimmer is the eel, whose snake-like body allows it to **undulate** quietly through small places in search of food. How did your fish swim?

Fish Camouflage

Tropical fish are **camouflage** geniuses. Sure, you might be able to see their bright colors and wild colors from a million miles away, but you're not a fish, are you? The secret to understanding fish camouflage is to see like a fish. And nobody's really quite figured out how to do that yet.

Scientists do know that fish don't see within the same light spectrum as people do. First of all, they're always underwater, and water filters out almost all colors of the light spectrum except for blue-greens. That means fish see blue-green colors particularly well, but yellows they don't really see at all. A yellow fish will disappear against the background of a coral reef.

But lots of tropical fish have blue-green stripes and other colors on them. These colors might not be for camouflage. They may be important in communicating with other fish, saying everything from, "Hey! Don't eat me. You'll regret it if you do," to, "We're the same species. Why don't you come hang out with me?"

For an activity on fish vision, turn to page 19.

Whiskers

Build an obstacle course and see how your cat uses those funky hairs on either side of his nose.

What You Need

- Boxes
- Books
- Your cat
- Tasty kitty treats (optional)

What You Do

1. Set up the books and boxes next to each other to create a corridor for your cat to walk through. Vary the size of the corridor so that some places it's wide and some places it's really narrow.

2. Bring your cat into the room. Watch what he does. Can he squeeze through the obstacles? Does he try? If he's totally uninterested in the obstacles, see whether you can tempt him through with a treat or two.

3. Reward your cat, even if he didn't play along. If he enjoyed the game, prop a book up so that it creates a triangle. Will your cat crawl through?

What's Going On?

Did your cat walk tall through the corridor? Did he hunker down and crawl through the narrow spaces? Cats don't have **whiskers** just because whiskers look cool. Those long hairs on their cheeks (also called **vibrissae**) grow to just the right length so a cat can test whether he can fit into (and also escape from) a space. There are special **sensory cells** in the skin at the base of each whisker. When a whisker touches an object, the cells release chemicals that give the cat's brain information about his surroundings. That's how your cat knew which passages he could fit through. Each cat's whiskers are unique. They increase in length as the cat grows from a kitten to an adult. If a whisker falls out naturally, a new one will grow in its place. Don't ever trim your cat's whiskers.

Know Your Nose

Dogs have noseprints instead of fingerprints.

What You Need

- Food coloring
- Paper towels
- As many dogs as you can find
- Small pad of paper
- Damp washcloth

What You Do

1. Use a clean paper towel to dry your dog's nose. Dab her nose gently—don't rub back and forth. Pour some of the food coloring onto another paper towel.

2. Dab the paper towel with the food coloring onto your dog's nose.

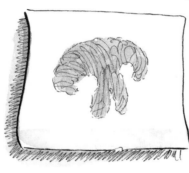

3. Gently press the pad of paper against your dog's nose. Don't press hard, but make sure you get your dog's entire nose. (Try bending the pad to get the sides of the nose.) You should see an impression on the pad.

4. Use a damp washcloth to wash the food coloring gently off your dog's nose. Give her a treat for playing along.

5. Repeat steps 1 through 4 for each dog.

6. Compare the nose prints you've collected. How are they similar? How are they different?

What's Going On?

A healthy dog's nose feels cool and wet, but did you ever notice the **ridges** in a dog's nose flesh? Those ridges are just like the ones on your fingertips, and just as unique. When you dab the food coloring onto your dog's nose, the food coloring gets into the curves formed in those ridges. It's just like inking your fingers for a **fingerprinting**. What shapes can you see in the nose prints?

Because each dog's nose is like no one else's, some **kennel clubs** and insurance companies accept nose prints as proof of a dog's identity. Even though your dog's nose is special, don't forget to have her always wear a **collar** with her name and your family's (or vet's office's) contact information, in case she gets lost. **Microchipping** is also a great way to identify your pet. (A microchip can't fall off or be easily removed by a pet thief.)

Sour Puss

Sweet or sour? Experiment with flavored waters to discover which your cat prefers.

What You Need

- Your cat
- Five small, clean bowls
- Tap water
- Sugar
- Lemon juice
- Tonic water

What You Do

1. Fill the bowls with tap water.

2. Add a bit of sugar to one, put a dash of lemon juice in another, and a splash of tonic water in the third bowl. Leave one bowl with plain, fresh tap water.

3. Set the bowls out for your cat, in order (standing water, sugar water, lemon water, tonic water, fresh water). Observe her to see which one she drinks out of first. What does she do with the others?

What's Going On?

Your cat, unless she's got some unusual tastes, probably went for the lemon water. Cats generally prefer salty or sour tastes, like most **carnivores**. They have trouble digesting sugar, and often end up with diarrhea if they do, so your cat probably avoided the sweet water. Scientists believe that cats can't actually taste sweets. The scientists theorize that cats lack a taste bud receptor for sweetness.

Try this experiment with your dog. He'll probably lap up all the sugar water. Dogs are well known for having a sweet tooth. Neither your cat nor your dog will go near the bitter-tasting tonic water.

He's so repulsive.

Yummy Toilet Water

Why do dogs drink out of the toilet?

What You Need

- Your dog
- Two small, clean bowls
- Tap water

What You Do

1. Fill one bowl with cool tap water. Let it stand for about an hour. (This will make it like the clean toilet bowl water your dog probably loves to drink.)

2. Fill the second bowl with cool tap water. Immediately present both bowls to your dog. Which one does she drink from first? Repeat this test each hour for 3 hours.

What's Going On?

Did your dog consistently choose the standing water? Does your dog also like to drink out of puddles, or the toilet? Scientists have different theories for why dogs have these preferences. One explanation is based on the **sense** of **taste**. People have more than 10,000 **taste buds** and can identify the **minerals**, **chemicals**, and other substances in water. When water stands, the substances settle at the bottom, or **evaporate**. To people, this water tastes stale. But dogs, though they have less than 2,000 taste buds, can recognize the taste of water itself. So dogs may choose standing water because it tastes pure. Another possible explanation is a lot simpler: does the water in the toilet get changed more often than the water in your dog's dish? The toilet gets fresh, clean water between six and ten times a day. How often does your dog get clean water? What other factors could you test to reveal why your dog drinks toilet water?

Spy on Your Dog

Be an ethologist for the day.

What You Need

- Your dog
- Paper and pencil
- Watch
- Your amazing powers of observation

What You Do

1. Follow your dog around and see what she does.

2. Write down what she does and the time at which she does it. Use the behaviors from the Doggy Deeds list on the next page to get started. Be as specific as possible. Be sure to include other circumstances, such as " sat down while getting fed, barked while meeting another dog," etc.

3. Analyze your data.

What's Going On?

Ethologists are scientists who study animals in their natural habitat to see how the animals react to different circumstances. Your dog's natural habitat is your home, so what she does is suited to her unique environment. What did you learn about her?

DOGGY DEEDS

- ✔ Sleeping
- ✔ Lying on side
- ✔ Lying on stomach
- ✔ Lying on back
- ✔ Rolling over
- ✔ Sitting
- ✔ Walking
- ✔ Running
- ✔ Scratching
- ✔ Stretching
- ✔ Yawning
- ✔ Chewing
- ✔ Drinking
- ✔ Licking
- ✔ Barking
- ✔ Growling
- ✔ Howling
- ✔ Whining
- ✔ Sniffing
- ✔ Curling up lip
- ✔ Squinting eyes
- ✔ Folding down ears
- ✔ Cocking ears
- ✔ Holding head high
- ✔ Slinking
- ✔ Wagging tail slowly
- ✔ Wagging tail quickly
- ✔ Wagging tail in a circle
- ✔ Tucking tail
- ✔ Raising hackles
- ✔ Chasing
- ✔ Biting

Aha!

Why do dogs chase cars? Most **animal behaviorists** agree that it's **instinct**. Dogs' bodies are hard-wired to react to moving objects and animals by running after them—even if their brains would normally warn them that chasing the moving parts on a 2-ton hunk of steel isn't a safe way to have a good time. This instinct developed because dog ancestors had to hunt down every meal. The chase instinct is so strong that many wild **predators** won't react to prey that is holding still. Now that dogs are **domesticated**, the chasing isn't necessary. But it sure looks like fun.

Mind Games

Test your dog's intelligence.

What You Need

- Low piece of furniture
- Your dog
- Doggy treat
- Stopwatch

What You Do

1. Find a low piece of furniture, low enough for your dog to stick her paw, but not her head, beneath.

2. Let your dog watch as you put her treat beneath the furniture. Start the stopwatch.

3. Time how long it takes her to get the treat with her paw.

4. If your dog enjoyed this, do the experiment again. This time, watch which paw your dog uses to get the treat. Is your dog right- or left-pawed?

What's Going On?

You watched your pet think and work through a problem. Her first solution, to pick up the treat with her mouth, didn't work. So she had to figure out a different way to get the treat. How many different solutions did she try? Look at the (unscientific!) scale below to rate your dog's intelligence in terms of how quickly she figured out the solution. Even if your dog doesn't score well on this test, she still has many qualities that make her a great companion.

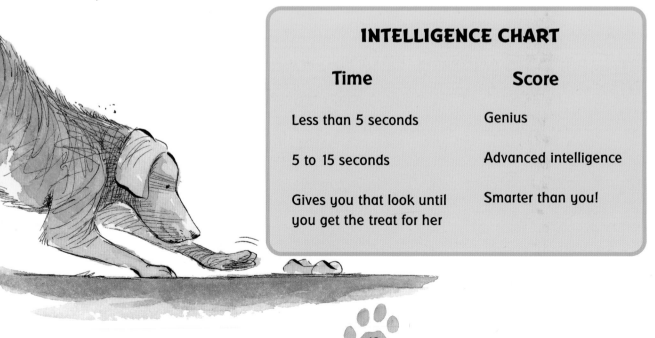

INTELLIGENCE CHART

Time	Score
Less than 5 seconds	Genius
5 to 15 seconds	Advanced intelligence
Gives you that look until you get the treat for her	Smarter than you!

Amaze Me

Time how quickly your dog can conquer a simple maze.

What You Need

- Cardboard
- Your dog
- Tape
- Adult helper
- Craft knife
- Doggy treat

What You Do

1. Stand the cardboard up on its side. Make it into a U-shape. The sides should be tall enough to make it impossible for your dog to jump over and longer than your dog's body. Use the tape if you need to add more pieces of cardboard.

2. Have your adult helper cut a hole in the bottom of the U shape, at the right height for your dog to see through the hole.

3. Convince your dog to get inside the U shape. Stand on the outside and hold a treat right at the hole. Tell her to come and get it.

4. How long does it take your dog to come around the outside of the U to where you are?

5. Try this experiment several times. Does your dog get better at the game with practice?

What's Going On?

This is another fun test for how your dog thinks. Your dog has to figure out that she has to walk away from the treat to get closer to it. Refer to the chart on page 48 to rate your dog's intelligence. Remember, even if your dog isn't quick to figure out the mind games you've set up, she's got more doggy smarts than any person.

TIME HER!

This Is Your Last Warning

Will your cat react to your invisible touch?

What You Need

- Your cat
- A comfortable place to rest
- A straw (optional)

What You Do

1. Sit or lie next to your cat, and let him get comfortable. Make sure that your face is no less than 1 foot from your cat, and that you and your cat aren't facing one another.

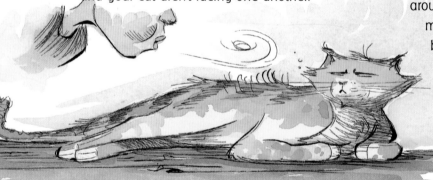

2. When your cat is relaxed and not paying particular attention to you, select a spot on his body and very gently blow a gentle breeze of air there. (You could blow through a straw instead, in which case you must blow even softer.) Do not blow anywhere near your cat's face or ears.

3. What was your cat's reaction? If you blew gently enough, he may not have noticed. If so, wait 1 full minute and then repeat. With each repetition, slightly increase the force of your breath until your cat reacts.

What's Going On?

Your cat should have turned in the direction of your breath. That's because every hair of an animal's **fur** is connected to **sensory nerves** that send signals to his brain. Since animals have so much more body hair than you, they're quicker to notice the movement of air around them. Also, **instinct** compels animals to be aware of the environment and be alert, to protect them from possible danger.

Was your cat slow to react? He may have ignored it because he knows when he's home with you he's safe. If your cat did react, test how little air it takes to get his attention by increasing the distance you are from him, or by blowing more softly.

Pet Smarts

If your cat displays any of the warning signals from page 11, stop the experiment immediately. He's telling you loud and clear that he doesn't like it at all!

Favorite Friends

Some birds like only one person. Some birds like everybody.

What You Do

1. Sit quietly in the corner of the room with your bird. Let your bird get used to you being there. (Maybe he'll even forget you're there.)

2. Have different people come into the room one at a time and stand by his cage. Have them talk to your bird, trying to engage his attention.

3. Observe your bird's reactions. Does he fluff his feathers, stand up very straight, or make noise?

What's Going On?

Birds can demonstrate an immediate reaction—favorable or unfavorable—to certain people. If your bird is protective of you, he may feel threatened by other people who take your attention away from him. If your bird is very social, he may be friendly toward most everyone he sees. Birds may **pair bond** with one individual in the family and be especially affectionate to that person. This is natural because in the **wild**, many birds bond with one **mate** for their entire lives. Don't be unhappy if your bird has a favorite person who's not you—you can't always pick who you fall in love with!

How does your bird recognize you? If you enter the room in a costume or wearing dark sunglasses, how does your bird react?

Sleeping with the Fishes

Do fish sleep?

What You Do

1. Watch your fish at different times during the day and night.

2. Write down how active she is each time you observe her. Be specific about what she does. Is she floating near the surface of the water or near the bottom? Is she swimming quickly or slowly? Are her little fins moving?

3. Can you see any patterns to when your fish is more or less active? Do you think she might be sleeping during any of those times?

What's Going On?

There may be times when your fish moves around less, or floats at the bottom of her tank. Is she sleeping? Well, we don't really know. Vets and scientists are still debating whether fish sleep like people and land animals do. Fish don't have eyelids, so you can't tell they're asleep when they close their eyes. Fish do, however, seem to have periods of rest during which they float in one place, lean against a rock, or bury themselves in the mud.

Aha!

Why don't fish sink when they stop swimming? Because they have an internal lifejacket called a **swim bladder**. A swim bladder is a sack in your fish's **abdomen** that can fill with **gas**. It helps keep him afloat—both while he's swimming and while he's chilling. Your fish can change the amount of air in his swim bladder to adjust his **buoyancy** (how much he floats). But not every fish has a swim bladder. For instance, a shark doesn't have a swim bladder because his internal organs and body shape are designed to keep him afloat.

Hermit Crab Hermitage

How does a crab select a home that's just right?

What You Do

1. Bring the water to a boil in the saucepan, and boil the shells for 5 minutes. This will make them clean and sterile for your crab. Rinse the shells under cool running water, and then let them cool and dry completely.

2. Carefully check the shells for holes or cracks. Discard the damaged ones. Your crab won't want them. Look at the shapes of the shells, their openings, and the insides. Identify as many different characteristics as you can.

3. Put the shells in your hermit crab's cage. Does he climb inside one? For how long does he stay? Crabs tend to be **nocturnal**, so he may wait until nightime to investigate the shells.

What's Going On?

A crab is a **crustacean** with an **exoskeleton**, segmented body, and joined legs. His spiral abdomen is covered by soft skin. It dries out quickly if he doesn't stay in a shell. So as a crab grows, he constantly seeks bigger shells to fit him. He generally prefers a shell that he can withdraw his whole body into, which provides the best protection from the **elements** and **predators**. Some crabs prefer an oval opening, because it's comfortable. Fit—not appearance—is the primary consideration when choosing a new shell.

Despite their name, hermit crabs crave companionship. Your crab should always have at least one hermit crab buddy to live and play with. To learn more about your pet crab, talk to your vet.

HOME 4-SALE

Salamander Spying

Discover how your salamander spends her days.

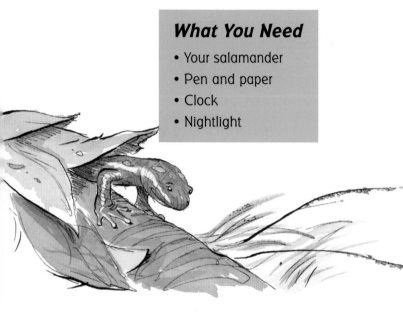

What You Need

- Your salamander
- Pen and paper
- Clock
- Nightlight

What You Do

1. Set up an observation post. Picking the right spot is essential. Make sure you can see most of the areas of your salamander's living space comfortably. Do not disturb or pry into your pet's private space.

2. Observe your salamander, making note of what she does at different times of day. (At night, use only a nightlight to observe her.) When is she in the water? When does she hang out on land? What sorts of things does she do when she's in both places?

3. Take detailed notes of your observations.

What's Going On?

Did your **salamander** hide out during the day and run around at night? Salamanders are generally active at night, and on rainy days (in the **wild**). This is because they have soft, **porous** skin that dries out quickly, so they have to avoid the sun and heat. During the day, salamanders hide in damp, dark areas, such as under logs and in leaf piles. They're **carnivorous** and prefer to hunt at night, eating certain insects, worms, spiders, slugs, and even other salamanders. Other **amphibians** share these qualities. **Toads** and **frogs** have porous skin and live near water, where they can find lots of insects to eat. Do you ever confuse salamanders with their reptile cousins, the **lizards**? Just remember that lizards have **scales** and prefer hot, dry environments.

Pet Smarts

Salamanders have soft skin that's easily damaged and quickly absorbs the oil from your hands—plus any germs, lotions, etc. These can make a salamander ill. So keep your hands to yourself! If you must touch your salamander, wash and dry your hands first.

Snake's Tongue

Find out why your snake is sticking out her tongue at you.

What You Need

- Cotton balls
- Bait or pet store that sells fish
- Re-sealable plastic bag
- Perfume
- Your dog or cat
- Feta cheese (optional)
- Your snake

What You Do

1. The first thing you're going to do is make the cotton balls smell like different things. Go to the bait store. Dip a cotton ball in a fish tank. Then squeeze out the excess water. Seal the cotton ball in the plastic bag.

2. Spray another cotton ball with perfume, and rub one cottonball on your dog or cat. If you have feta cheese, put a spoonful in a small dish. Fill the dish with water and let it set for 10 minutes. Dip a cotton ball into the cheese-water, and then squeeze it out.

3. Place the scented and dipped cotton balls, one at a time, in your snake's cage. Count how many times your snake flicks her tongue at each cotton ball.

What's Going On?

Did your snake flick her tongue at the cotton balls? She wasn't licking them. A snake smells with both her nose and her tongue. She flicks her tongue out, collecting floating odor **particles**, and then presses her tongue to the roof of her mouth. This transfers the particles to her **vomeronasal organ**, located near her nasal passages. At the same time, she inhales odor particles, drawing them into the **olfactory chamber**. Both the vomeronasal organ and the olfactory chamber send information to the brain, which identifies the odors. Snakes use their sense of smell to find and identify **prey**, **navigate** through the environment, and find a **mate**.

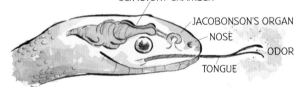

OLFACTORY CHAMBER

JACOBONSON'S ORGAN

NOSE

ODOR

TONGUE

Aha!

Amphibians and **reptiles** are **wild** creatures. Unlike **domesticated animals**, they aren't bred to be companions for you. If you want one for a pet, make sure you learn a lot about them. Ask your vet what kind of **environment** each animal needs to be happy, and provide a vet-approved diet.

Sherlock the Rat Detective

Watch your pet deduce the best route through a cool bottle maze.

What You Need

- Empty and clean plastic soda bottles*
- Scissors
- Craft knife
- Adult helper
- Tape
- Treat
- Stopwatch
- Your rat

* Make sure that your rat can easily fit through the bottles.

What You Do

1. You'll use the soda bottles to make a maze for your rat. Cut the tops off the plastic bottles with the scissors. Have an adult use the craft knife to make three dime-size airholes in each bottle you use, plus a large hole in one or two sides of some of the bottles. The sideholes should be as wide as the hole in the tops of the bottles, so you can create passageways like you see in the maze on the right. Cut away the bottoms of some of the plastic bottles, but leave some of the bottoms on to make dead ends.

2. Construct a maze from the bottles, taking care to have the airholes on top. If the bottles don't fit together just right, tape them together. Leave two openings as a start and a finish, as shown in the maze on the next page.

3. Place the treat at the finish. Put your rat at the start. Time how long it takes her to find the treat. Repeat the process, placing the treat and your rat in exactly the same places as before. Does her time improve?

What's Going On?

Your rat probably made it through the maze more quickly each time you put her in it. Rats are really, really intelligent, and they learn things through **repetition**. The more often you put your rat in the maze, the more quickly she'll figure out how to get through it.

This is one of the main reasons that scientists have used rats as experimental test subjects for hundreds of years. (Hmm. Sometimes it doesn't pay to be smart!)

Rats need lots of stimulation to keep them from getting bored. They like everything from mazes to toys. Parrot, gerbil, and hamster toys are all suitable playthings for rats. But forget about the hamster wheel! Rats are smart enough to figure out that they won't get anywhere on that thing. Rats really enjoy using their brains for problem solving. Cardboard boxes and toilet paper tubes will keep your rat entertained (and playing architect) for weeks.

Rats are also very social animals. They thrive when they have at least one rat roommate and get depressed when living alone. Rats also live longer if they are able to enjoy the company of other rats. If you have a rat who is used to living by herself, talk your vet about the best way to introduce her to a companion.

cut here

clear tape

What, Swiss again!?

Seeing Is Believing

You know your dog can smell better than you, but does your dog see better too?

What You Need

- Pirate eye patch (optional)
- Your dog

What You Do

1. Put on the eye patch so it covers one of your eyes. (If you don't have an eye patch, use your hand to cover your eye.)

2. Follow your dog around on your knees (or at about her height), right behind her. (She may just turn around and stare at you at first. Be patient. It may take a minute for her to understand that you're going to follow her around.) Don't move your head unless your dog moves her head, too.

3. What did you bump into? Reward your dog for playing along.

What's Going On?

You probably banged into a few things, but your dog didn't have this problem. That's because even though you and your dog have similar **vision**, your dog has two super senses.

Dogs and people both have **binocular vision**—the eyes are placed on the front of the head, rather than on the sides. So, this means dogs and people have similar abilities to see what's in front of them and what's on either side. Dogs may, however, notice objects sooner than you because their senses of hearing and smell are so much more advanced than ours.

A-Ha!

Have you noticed that most dogs don't approach each other head on and don't stare at one another? In dog **body language**, these actions would be perceived as **aggressive**. That's because dogs are **pack animals**, and this means they have to establish who is **top dog.** In the wild, the top dog makes all the decisions about where and when the pack eats, sleeps, and so on.

When two dogs meet, often the more **dominant** dog will look directly at the other dog. The less dominant dog will look away, or even lie on the ground. This indicates **submission**. If one dog refuses to submit, there may be a scuffle or even an all-out fight. The purpose is to establish who is top dog. It's normal for dogs to behave this way, but that's also why you should keep your dog on a leash when you leave the house together. You need to protect your pet from other animals—and from her own instincts!

Did You Hear That?

Dogs can hear things that you can't.

What You Do

1. Watch your dog in a large, secure area. Stand at least 6 feet away. Let your dog forget you're there.

2. Blow the whistle. Watch how your dog reacts. Did you hear anything?

3. Test your dog's reaction when you blow the whistle while standing in three different locations: in front, behind, and beside her.

What's Going On?

Dogs have excellent hearing. Their ears are designed to hear higher **frequencies** and lower volumes than people can. That's part of how they may know when storms are coming and how they know you are home before you even get inside the house. (See pages 34 and 35.) Dogs who have ears that stand up are said to hear better than dogs with floppy ears. (Makes sense, doesn't it?) Dogs' ears are shaped to catch sounds, just as you can when

you cup your hands behind your ears to hear better. Also, dogs can rotate their ears to stretch and pick up sounds. (So can horses and many other animals.)

Pet Smarts

Only use dog whistles for this experiment and for training routines recommended by your vet. The sound can become annoying and cause your dog discomfort. (These whistles are used with hunting and herding dogs, to alert the dogs without scaring away **prey** or **livestock**.)

Cat in a Bag

To you, it's just a paper bag, but to your cat it's a lot more.

Pet Smarts

Keep plastic bags out of reach of your cat, such as in a drawer. Like a child, a cat could easily get a plastic bag stuck on his head and suffocate.

What You Do

1. Lay out the paper bag.

2. Watch your cat investigate the bag. Does he get near it? How near? Does he go inside? What does he do in there?

3. When your cat seems to be tired of the bag, replace it with the box.

4. Watch how your cat responds to the box. How is his behavior similar to and different from his response to the bag?

What's Going On?

Paper bags are convenient caves for your cat to hide in. This allows him to act out his natural hunting **instinct** by waiting for unsuspecting prey to walk by. (Your other cat, a toy, and your foot are all **prey** in this game.) Cats love to feel that they are out of sight and have the ability to surprise you when they jump out of the bag. Your cat probably played in the bag, but was less interested in the cardboard box. That's because boxes tend to be less cave-like, so they aren't as much fun to hide in.

The Literate Cat

Does your cat prefer newspapers, magazines, or books?

What You Need

- A newspaper
- A magazine
- A book
- A table or bed your cat is allowed on
- A chair
- Your cat

What You Do

1. Place the newspaper, magazine, and book on the table, about a foot apart from one another.

2. Move to the other side of the room and watch your cat. Does he investigate the things on the table?

3. Pick up the newspaper, sit down, and begin reading. Observe your cat's reaction. Then exchange the newspaper for the magazine, and observe your cat. Do the same with the book.

What's Going On?

Unless you read often, your cat may not have been interested in the reading materials on the table. But when your cat lies on something you are using (or reading), your cat is saying that he sees what you are interested in, and he wants you to transfer your attention to him. Pronto!

Howls, Yowls, and Meows

Figure out what makes your pet "talk"
— and what she's saying.

Knock, Knock

What You Need

- Your pet
- A friend
- A room

1. The friend, you, and your pet, should meet in the room. Have the friend gently talk to and pet your pet. The friend should then leave the room, shut the door, and quietly stand nearby.

2. You should get comfortable, so you and your pet can relax. After a minute, the friend should knock lightly on the door. You ignore it. Observe your pet, without being obvious. Is she noticing the sound? How can you tell?

3. After another minute, the friend should knock again, louder. Continue to ignore the sound and watch your pet. What does she do?

4. End the activity by opening the door for your friend. Reward your pet for her behavior, and make sure she sees that the person knocking was just the friend she met a few minutes ago.

What's Going On?

Most likely, your pet looked in the direction of the knocking, and then looked back at you. She may have even gone to the door, or to your side, to get your attention. Since you continued to ignore the sound, your pet probably took the next step and tried to alert you with her voice. She said, "Hey, don't you hear that? Shouldn't you see who's knocking?" Staying alert is a natural safety **instinct** for animals, and for people too. Your pet thinks of you as part of her family, and she's watching out for you.

Feed Me!

What You Need

- Your pet
- Your pet's regular feeding schedule
- Pet bowl
- Pet food

What You Do

1. You should be feeding your pet at regular times each day, so your pet isn't ever hungry and always knows when he'll eat his next meal. At his next mealtime, go with your pet to the place where you feed him and get out his food bowl. Don't put anything in it. Instead, put down the empty dish and get comfortable—as if you are just there to hang out.

2. Observe your pet's behavior. What is he doing?

3. After a minute, take your pet's food bowl and put in the correct amount of food. Now put the food bowl out of the pet's reach, and get comfortable again.

4. Observe your pet. What's he doing now?

5. End the activity by rewarding your pet for being your test subject. Now feed him!

What's Going On?

Did your pet do something to get your attention? When you set the food out of his reach, did he redouble his efforts? Did he sit or stand beside the bowl and "talk" to you? You tested your pet's ability to **communicate** his **food desire**. Food is a necessity for life, and most pets aren't shy about letting you know this. Chances are, your pet did talk. He said, "Feed me!" When you didn't respond, he added, "Pretty please? Huh? Pretty pretty please?"

Mee-oww

Look at Me!

What You Do

1. You should have a daily routine of when and how you relax with and play with your pet each day, so your pet isn't starved for your attention. At the next special time with your pet, instead of touching or talking to your pet, ignore her. Also, don't make any eye contact with your pet! (This can be hard to do, but the experiment won't last too long!)

2. Observe your pet's behavior. What is she doing?

3. After a minute, change your position (stand if you were sitting, sit if you were standing), and continue to ignore your pet.

4. Observe your pet. What's she doing now?

5. End the activity by rewarding your pet with petting, praise, and a smile.

What's Going On?

Your attention is very important to your pet. In fact, the desire for your **companionship** is one of the few things in the world that will compel a pet to "talk" to you! Did your pet touch you, bring you a toy, or try looking you in the eye and making noise? If so, she was reminding you that she's your friend and she'd like to spend some time with you. If your pet didn't mind you ignoring her, you two need to spend more quality time together, so she knows she can count on you to always be her friend.

Pet Smarts

It's easy to fit in several five-minute segments of play or relaxation—petting, holding—each and every day. Just make time around your schedule for getting up in the morning, doing chores, doing homework, and so on. If you have a dog, you also need to spend a half-hour or more each day going for a walk or doing another form of exercise with him.

Purrrrr...

Ever wonder how and why cats **purr**? Cats have a body part that makes it possible. Most cats have a fold of vocal tissue in their throats called the **vocal fold**. With their mouths shut, cats send air over the vocal fold and make the murmuring **vibration** we call purring. This is true for most **domestic** cats, and some big cats. Mountain lions, pumas, and cheetahs purr, for instance, but tigers can't.

There are lots of theories for the reasons cats purr. They often do it when they are content and happy, but sometimes they do it when they're nervous or injured. Kittens begin purring when they are just a few days old. Some scientists think that purring helps cats to heal from their injuries.

Scientists theorize that raccoons also purr. Have you heard other kinds of animals purr?

What's in an Eye?

Make your cat's eyes change size and color.

What You Do

1. Get on your hands and knees so that your face is level with your cat's face. Using your amazing powers of observation, check out the shape and size of his pupils. (The pupil is the dark part of the eye.)

2. Turn off the lights.

3. Wait a minute, and then look at your cat's pupils again by putting the penlight a few inches from his face and shining the penlight in his eyes. The pupils should be huge, but within a few seconds the pupils will shrink to an even smaller size than they were in the lighted room. Also check out the shiny green or yellow reflection in the back of his eyes.

4. You can turn on the light and reward your cat with a tasty treat for letting you play **optometrist**. Or leave the lights off and let him chase the beam of light from the pen—shine it on the floor or walls.

What's Going On?

In order to see and recognize **visual images**, the **retina** (the back of the eye where the visual receptors are) must have an appropriate amount of light available. This is true for every kind of eye—human, **feline**, **canine**, etc. The **pupil** (the colored dot in the center of an eye) lets in the light. It **dilates** in low light (to take

In Normal Light

In the Dark

Light Reaction

in more light) and **contracts** in bright light (to limit the light). That's why your cat's pupils widened, and then shrunk.

Because cats are **nocturnal** animals, their eyes contain a **reflective** layer called the **tapetum**. The tapetum magnifies tiny amounts of light—allowing cats to see at night and in the dark. You can see the tapetum: It's the shiny green or yellow reflection in the back of your cat's eyes.

Night Vision

Animals don't all see the same colors you do, but they don't see in black and white either. Instead, they can see as well as they need to—and some see better than you do in the dark.

All eyes work the same way: Light passes through the **pupil** and **iris** and is focused by the **lens** onto the **retina** at the back of the eye, a bit like a movie projector focuses light onto a screen. The retina is the part of the eye that processes light and sends images to the brain. It's lined with special **cells** called **cones** and **rods**.

Cones help see color and **details** but need medium or bright light to function. Some eyes, such as human eyes, are **diurnal** (built for daylight). They rely on the cones a lot. Daylight eyes see a colorful world, so you can recognize lots of shades.

Rods are just the opposite: They don't work in bright light, and they can't detect color or detail. But in dim light, they gradually absorb a special chemical called **rhodopsin**. Once they've absorbed enough rhodopsin, they can send signals about

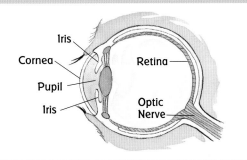

motion, basic shapes, and shades of gray to the brain. Some eyes, such as those of cats, owls, and raccoons, are **nocturnal** (built for darkness). They rely more on the rods, and some nocturnal animals have very few or no cones. Nocturnal eyes see in the dark because they translate what they see into many, many shades of gray.

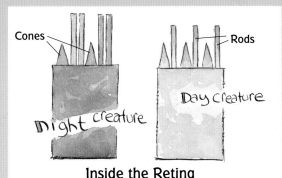

Inside the Retina

Can You Say What I Say?

If you've got a little patience and an outgoing parrot, you can teach him to talk to you.

Good Morning

What You Need

- Your parrot
- Patience

3. The best time for you to teach your parrot to talk is in the morning or at dusk. Pick a simple one or two word phrase for your bird to learn. It will help if there is an action to go with the word. For instance, you could say "Good morning!" as you take the cover off his cage. Repeat this often. Do not change what you say, even a little bit.

4. Work with your parrot for 10 to 20 minutes every day for at least two weeks. At this point, your parrot may start to imitate you. Usually he'll do this in private, until he knows he can make the sounds right.

What You Do

1. Make sure your parrot is happy, healthy, and comfortable in his surroundings. If your parrot is nervous, he won't want to talk. If you've just adopted a parrot, let him get used to being a part of your family for at least a week before beginning this experiment.

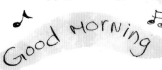

Good Morning

2. Get rid of all distractions. Turn of the TV, music, computers, and clear the room of other pets and family members. This will make it easier for you and your parrot to concentrate.

What's Going On?

Parrots are really talented **mimics**. They can imitate almost any sound they hear. When you teach your parrot to talk, you're teaching him to imitate the sounds you make. (That's why it's so important to repeat the same word in the exact same way.) If you want your parrot to learn a long phrase, sentence, or even nursery rhyme, break the phrase into smaller pieces and teach them to him slowly.

Parrots don't have vocal cords. Instead, they use their throat muscles, directing the airflow so it produces certain sounds. (That's why your parrot likes to practice in private!) Some parrots learn to imitate lots of different sounds around them—not just human voices. There are parrots that sound like telephones, printers, fax machines, and the radio.

Sometimes parrots don't talk. If you have two (or more) birds, they'll probably talk (in parrot-speak) to each other. Males talk a lot more than females generally. It's also easier to teach birds who are between two and three months old to talk than it is to teach older birds. If your parrot is adamant about not talking, you could try to teach him to whistle your favorite song.

People don't agree on whether or not parrots understand the meaning of the words they're saying. Some people say that parrots do know what they're saying. Others just think that the parrots are imitating the sounds they've heard.

Pet Smarts

Don't take your parrot act on the road. Unless your parrot is a freak of nature, he will not enjoy speaking in front of people. Don't practice or ask him to talk when there are strangers around (a stranger being anybody who doesn't live with you and your bird.) He probably won't. If he wants to talk to strangers, let him decide when to do it and what to say.

Parrots That Will Probably Talk

These birds are known for being loudmouths.

- African Grey
- Budgie
- Macaw
- Conure
- Eclectus
- Cockatoo

Parrots That Might Talk

These birds can be a little shy, but they'll talk if they've got something to say.

- Pionus
- Poicephalus
- Parrotlets
- Lovebirds

Give Your Pet a Hug

How does your pet express affection?

What You Do

1. Sit near your cat or dog while he is relaxing.

2. Stretch out your hand. Hold it within your pet's reach until he reacts.

3. What does your pet do?

4. Try stretching out your foot, your nose, your chin, and other body parts. Does your pet react differently to these?

What's Going On?

Did your cat rub on your arm? How about any other parts of your body? It may be more than just wanting to be petted. Cats have **scent glands** on their back, **muzzle,** forehead, and neck. When your cat rubs these parts of his body against you, he's depositing his scent on you. Other cats will smell his scent and know that you two belong to each other.

Did your dog nuzzle into the palm of your hand? Your dog's behavior has to do with being a **pack animal.** She saw your outstretched hand as an invitation to get some attention from the **pack alpha** (you!), so of course she took you up on the offer.

Primates (monkeys, apes, and humans) all hug each other to show affection and be comforted. Some scientists speculate that primates hug because it brings their hearts close together.

Wag the Dog

Figure out what makes your dog happy.

What You Need

- Pencil and paper
- Paper bag
- Dog toys
- Balls
- Leash
- Brush
- Peanut butter jar
- Dog food
- Dog treats
- Your dog

What You Do

1. With the pencil and paper, make a chart listing each of the items, leaving room for you to write down your dog's reaction to each one. Put the items in the paper bag.

2. Sit or stand near your dog and the items. Have your dog sit or lie down, if she can.

3. Without speaking, take each item out of the bag and show it to your dog, and watch your dog's reaction. Make notes if she wags her tail, barks, ignores you, goes to sleep, etc. Only hold each item as long as needed to see her reaction. Don't punish or reward your dog for any behavior—just observe.

4. After testing each item, praise and pet your dog to thank her for being in the experiment.

What's Going On?

Your dog can't speak, so she **communicates** with you with her **body language**. So, as you showed her each item in the experiment, she reacted to let you know what that item made her think about and what she thinks about that activity.

A happy dog behaves in a way that encourages you to start or continue the activity she enjoys. For instance, if she likes to be brushed, she may push at your hand or the brush with her head, in hopes that you'll continue. An unhappy dog may crouch down on the ground, try to run away from you, or growl. This is her way of saying that she doesn't like an activity or wants to be left alone.

If your dog behaves unhappy often, talk to your vet. She may need medical attention or a new play and exercise program. In the meantime, spend some time indulging her in whatever she said is her favorite activity.

Make Your Bed

What makes a nest snuggle-worthy?

What You Need

- Toilet paper rolls
- Cardboard
- Wood chips* (not cedar or pine)
- Sticks* (not cedar or pine)
- Straw*
- Rags
- Your hamster, gerbil, rat, or guinea pig and his cage
- Coffee can or clay pot (optional)

* Find at a pet supply store

What You Do

1. Put the different nesting materials in your pet's cage. You could put a coffee can in the cage, for a **nest box**, if you want.

2. See which material he uses to make a nest. How does he choose a material? How does he make a nest?

What's Going On?

Your pet probably went right to work, because small rodents are driven to nest. (Hamsters often stuff their cheeks with food and bedding material to carry to their nests. Did yours?) This drive is called the **nesting instinct**. The nest provides protection from **predators**, a place to store food, and a place to rest—so, it makes sense for a rodent to have a good nest.

When you clean your pet's cage, remember to put the nest and any hidden food back where you found them. Otherwise, your pet will have to start all over again to get his nest just right.

Pet Smarts

Cedar and pine chips or sticks are **toxic** to your pet rodent. Don't ever use them. If you have trouble finding good materials to use for this activity, ask your vet for suggestions.

Wild Gerbils!

Your gerbil is a burrowing machine.

What You Need

- 4 large cardboard boxes
- Potting soil without additives
- Dirt from your yard
- Wood chips (not cedar or pine)
- Sand
- Masking tape
- Your gerbil

What You Do

1. Fill each of the cardboard boxes with a different type of burrowing material: potting soil, dirt from your yard, wood chips, and sand.

2. Arrange the boxes so that their flaps overlap on the outside (see illustration). Tape the flaps in place. These will make an area on which your gerbil can move from box to box.

3. Set your gerbil on the flaps of the cardboard box. Watch how he reacts to the different types of burrowing material. Is there one that he prefers?

What's Going On?

Your **gerbil** probably had a blast exploring all the different burrowing materials. The sand would have reminded him the most of his ancestral home, because gerbils are originally from the desert areas of Africa, Asia, and India. (Did your pet dig the sand best?) There are more than 100 different gerbil **species**. Most are between 6 and 12 inches long, from nose to tail. They are **adapted** to living in dry **climates** and burrow to protect themselves and their families from the **elements** and **predators**.

Sand   Dirt   Wood Chips   Potting Soil

Sleepytime Blues

Why do dogs walk in tight circles before lying down?

What You Need

- Your dog

What You Do

1. Watch your dog as she gets ready for bed. What does she do?

2. How do you know when she's asleep? Does she sleep with her eyes open or closed? Does she dream?

What's Going On?

Most likely, your dog turned around a few times before lying down. No one is really sure why dogs do this. There are several theories though. One of the most common is that dogs are responding to their **nesting instinct.** When your dog walks over the same area repeatedly, she's trampling the blankets, grass, or dirt to make a nice, comfortable place for her body. Another theory is that your dog turns around until her nose is pointed downwind. That way, she can smell anything dangerous approaching.

Animals have many different sleeping postures. Birds tuck their heads under their wings when sleeping. Newts and salamanders sleep beneath rocks and dead trees. Some animals close their eyes to sleep, while others sleep with their eyes open. Horses can sleep standing up, eyes closed. Animals sleep for different amounts of time as well. In general, larger mammals tend to sleep less than smaller ones. A hamster generally sleeps for more than 14 hours a day. A cat sleeps for about 12 hours, and a dog sleeps for about 10 hours. Horses sleep less than 3 hours a night. Scientists don't fully understand the ways that fish, insects, and reptiles sleep.

One good turn deserves another.

...And Now, A Brief Paws

We hope you and your pets had fun and got to know each other a little better by using this book. Now that you've had such a great start, don't ever stop exploring why your pets do the things they do! Play with your pets, pay attention to them, and you'll discover more amazing things about them every day.

P.S. If you loved this book, check out *Smash It! Crash It! Launch It! 50 Eye-Popping, Mind-Blowing Science Experiments*, in which Jessie schools her friends in rocket science as they make all sorts of everyday objects crunch, smash, soar, and more.

Or, look for *Chemistry Concoctions: 50 Formulas that Fizz, Foam, Splatter & Ooze,* in which the kids turn Lucinda's garage into a chemistry lab. And of course, there's *It's Not Magic, It's Science! 50 Science Tricks that Mystify, Dazzle & Astound,* in which Tim teaches his friends to perform amazing science tricks that work like magic. There aren't any pets in these books, but they're still fun.

Glossary

Abdomen. the part of the body that contains an animal's stomach, intestines, and other vital organs.

Adaptation. a change made so that an animal is better equipped to survive in specific circumstances.

Aggressive. exhibiting hostile behavior or action.

Alert. to make someone aware of something.

Allergic reaction. an abnormal and negative response to food or something in the environment.

Amphibian. a cold-blooded animal that lays eggs and lives in the water when young, but moves to land and breathes air when grown.

Amputate. to cut off a body part.

Animal behaviorist. a person who studies how an animal acts in its environment.

Animal shelter. a place that gives animals who need homes basic shelter, food, and medical attention.

Attention. concentration on something or somebody.

Avian. belonging to the family of birds.

Backbone. the spine.

Barb. one of the hair-like branches on the shaft of a feather, or a sharp hook pointing backward.

Behavioral science. the study of an animal's actions in response to its environment.

Binocular vision. using both eyes to see.

Biologist. a scientist who studies biology.

Biology. the study of life and all living organisms.

Bipedal. an animal that walks on two legs.

Bird. a warm-blooded, egg-laying animal, with feathers, wings, and a bill.

Black light bulb. a light bulb that produces ultraviolet light.

Blow a coat. to shed an outer coat of fur all at once.

Body fat. food stored in the body to keep an animal warm and act as an emergency source of energy.

Body heat. the temperature generated by metabolism and given off as heat.

Body language. postures and facial expressions that communicate a feeling or mood.

Bred. when two animals are mated in order to produce offspring with specific characteristics.

Breed. a group of animals with common characteristics and ancestors.

Brown fat. a type of fat found in newborn and hibernating mammals.

Buoyancy. having the quality of being buoyant.

Buoyant. able to float in water.

Camouflage. coloring and/or patterns that disguise an animal.

Canine. belonging to the family that includes dogs and wolves.

Carnivore. an animal that feeds primarily on the flesh of other animals.

Carnivorous. an animal that follows the diet of a carnivore.

Cat. carnivorous mammal with sharp, retractable claws and soft fur.

Catnip. a plant that attracts cats.

Cecum. the first part of the large intestine.

Cell. the basic unit of living matter.

Chemical. a substance created by a chemical process.

Chemistry. the study of the structure, properties, and reactions of chemical elements and the compounds they form.

Chew toys. toys designed specifically to exercise an animal's teeth, gums, and jaws.

Claws. the sharp curved nails on the toes of a mammal, reptile, or bird.

Climate. the general weather condition of an area.

Coat. the fur or hair of an animal.

Cold blooded. an animal whose body temperature changes according to the surrounding temperature.

Collar. the one article of clothing that a dog or cat should always wear.

Color vision. the ability to perceive different wavelengths of light as color.

Comfort. to soothe.

Communicate. to express something so that someone else understands it.

Companionship. friendship.

Cones. the cone-shaped cells in the eye which are sensitive to color and bright light.

Constant. unchanging.

Contract. to get smaller.

Crustacean. an animal that has a hard shell and lives mostly in water.

Dander. dandruff.

Dandruff. tiny particles of dried skin that fall off in flakes, sometimes visible in hair, fur, or feathers.

Declaw. amputation of the claws from an animal's paws.

Details. small parts of the whole.

Digestive system. the system of organs that break down and absorb food.

Dilate. to get larger or expand.

Diurnal. more active in the daytime.

Displace. to take the space of.

Dog. carnivorous mammal with a fur coat, tail, and big wet tongue.

Domesticated. adapted, tamed, or trained to live and work with humans.

Dominant. the one who has the most influence, control, and the highest social status.

Dorsal fin. a fin on the back of the fish.

Drag. a friction-produced force that slows motion.

Elements. the weather.

Energy. the capacity for work or movement.

Environment. the physical or natural conditions of an area.

Equine. belonging to the family of horses.

Ethologist. a scientist who studies the behavior of an animal in its natural environment.

Evaporate. to change from a liquid state to a vapor.

Exoskeleton. a hard, protective covering on the outside of the body.

Extra-sensory perception. perception by means other than the five senses.

Fatal. deadly.

Feline. belonging to the family that includes cats, tigers, leopards, and lions.

Feral. a domesticated animal that has returned to living in an untamed, wild state.

Fermentation. a chemical reaction that breaks down complex compounds into simpler ones.

Fingerprinting. copying the pattern of ridges in the skin of the fingers in order to identify someone.

Food desire. hunger.

Footpads. the fleshy, padded parts of an animal's foot.

Frequency. the wavelength that a sound travels at.

Frog. an amphibian with smooth, moist skin and webbed feet.

Fur. thick, soft hair covering the body of a mammal.

Gas. one of the forms of matter that has no fixed shape or volume.

Gene. a segment of DNA that determines hereditary characteristics.

Gland. an organ that produces or secretes a specific substance, often a hormone.

Grooming. removing dirt, parasites, and dead fur from the coat of an animal.

Hair. a fine strand of fur that grows out of a mammal's skin.

Hay. dried grass, clover, alfalfa and other plants used to feed grazing animals.

Herbivore. an animal that eats plants.

Herd. a group of animals that live together.

Hormone. a chemical produced by the body that stimulates a certain action or reaction.

Horse. a large mammal with hooves, a coarse mane, and a tail.

Humane society. an organization dedicated to treating animals with mercy and compassion.

Hypoallergenic. not causing an allergic reaction.

Inedible. unable to be digested.

Instinct. a behavior that an animal is born with.

Instinctually. something done because of instinct.

Insulation. a covering that keeps an animal warm.

Intestinal tract. the part of the digestive system that extends from stomach to anus.

Iris. the colored part of the eye.

Kangaroo. an Australian mammal with short front legs and large, powerful hind legs.

Kennel club. an organization that registers information about dogs and their owners.

Keratin. a tough protein that forms the outer layers of hair, nails, horns, feathers, and hooves.

Land dwellers. creatures that live on land.

Lens. a transparent structure in the eye that focuses light on the retina.

Light spectrum. the range of wavelengths seen in light as different colors.

Livestock. animals raised on farms to work for humans.

Lizard. a reptile with a scaly, slender body and a long tail.

Locomotion. the act or ability to move from one place to another.

Long-term memory. the specific brain function that stores information for extended periods of time.

Mammal. a warm-blooded animal that gives birth to live babies.

Mat. a dense tangle of hair.

Mate. a bond two animals form in order to produce young, or the act of reproduction.

Metabolism. the process in which food is turned into energy.

Microchip. a computer chip encoded with information about a pet that is implanted beneath the dog or cat's skin. It can only be read by a special scanner.

Mimic. to copy or imitate.

Minerals. inorganic solids with a crystalline structure.

Muzzle. the mouth area of an animal.

Natural environment. the physical and biological conditions in which an animal developed.

Navigate. to plot a course.

Nepetalactone. the chemical in catnip that makes it so appealing to cats.

Nest box. a place for an animal to make a nest.

Nesting instinct. an animal's drive to make a safe and a comfy place to sleep for itself, its mate, and its young.

Nocturnal. most active at night.

Nutrients. the ingredients in food that nourish the body.

Observation. the act of watching.

Olfactory chamber. the organ that processes smell.

Opportunist. an animal that takes advantage of any situation to achieve a goal.

Optometrist. a doctor who studies eyes.

Organ. a particular part of an animal developed to perform a certain function.

Overweight. weighing more than normal.

Pack alpha. the leader of a group or family.

Pack animals. an animal that lives in a social group, like a big family.

Pair bond. when two animals are connected by strong emotional ties.

Particle. a speck of solid matter.

Pectoral fin. a fin on the chest or side of a fish.

Perch. a branch or rod that a bird uses for roosting.

Pheromones. a chemical secreted by one animal that influences the behavior of others.

Phosphor. a substance that shines in the dark without burning.

Porous. having tiny holes through which liquids and gasses can pass.

Posture. the position of a human or animal's body.

Predator. an animal that hunts other animals for food.

Predatory behavior. behavior exhibited by a predator, particularly when in hunting mode.

Prey. an animal hunted and caught for food.

Proportional. balance between all of the parts in a whole.

Protein. a complex organic chemical compound that forms the basis of living tissue.

Psychic. a person who knows things that he can't logically know.

Pupil. the opening in the middle of the iris that lets light into the eyeball.

Purr. the soft, vibrant sound a cat makes.

Quadruped. an animal that walks on four legs.

Rabbit. a burrowing mammal with soft hair, long ears, and strong, powerful hind legs.

Rabies. a fatal disease that infects mammals and is transmitted by bite.

Reflective. shining light back rather than absorbing it.

Repetition. an acting or event that happens over and over again.

Reptile. a cold-blooded, scaly animal that typically lays eggs.

Retina. a light-sensitive membrane in the back of the eye.

Retractable claw. a claw that can be drawn into the body.

Rhodopsin. a chemical found in the eye that allows an animal to see in dim light.

Ridge. a long, narrow raised area.

Rodent. a type of mammal that has large front teeth for gnawing.

Rods. the elongated cells in the retina that are sensitive to dim light.

Salamander. an animal that resembles a lizard but has smooth, moist skin.

Scales. the thin, overlapping plates that form the skin of fish, reptiles, and some other animals.

Scent glands. the glands that produce chemicals that other animals smell to discover information about the animal producing the chemicals.

Scratching post. a wooden post covered in carpet that cats scratch to remove old layers from their claws and exercise, or an object with a similar function.

Sense. the functions that allow an animal to perceive its environment.

Sensitive. very responsive to an external condition or stimulus.

Sensory cells. cells that receive and transmit the information given to them by the senses.

Sensory nerves. a bundle of fibers that carry sensory information through the body.

Shed. the natural process by which a mammal loses old pieces of fur or hair. (Humans shed too!)

Short-term memory. the specific brain function that stores information temporarily.

Skin coverings. the fur, feathers, or scales that cover the skin of an animal.

Specialized. developed or adapted to suit a particular environment.

Species. a group of animals that are the same kind and can produce offspring.

Stalk. to pursue prey quietly.

Submission. to surrender to a person or animal with more authority.

Swim bladder. the organ that allows a fish to float.

Tadpole. the larval stage of a frog or toad.

Tapetum. the iridescent membrane covering the back of the eye, mostly found in nocturnal animals.

Taste. the sense that distinguishes between different flavors.

Taste buds. rounded protuberances on the tongue that contain cells to distinguish between different flavors.

Tendon. a band of tissue that connects a muscle to a bone.

Terrain. the surface features of an area of land.

Toad. an animal that resembles a frog, but has drier, rougher skin and lives primarily on land when grown.

Top dog. the dominant dog in a pack.

Touch. to come in contact with something, or to feel with a part of the body.

Toxic. poisonous.

Traction. the friction between an animal's paw and the ground which allows the animal to move instead of sliding.

Trigger. a stimulus that sets off a reaction.

Ultraviolet light. a wavelength of light that is shorter than visible light.

Undercoat. a covering of short hair that lies beneath the longer fur.

Undulate. to move back and forth or up and down in a wave-like pattern, like the movement of a snake.

Vertebrae. the bones of the spine.

Veterinarian. a doctor for animals.

Vibration. fast rhythmic back and forth movement.

Vibrissae. the long, stiff hairs that grow near the mouth and nose, also called whiskers.

Vision. eyesight.

Visual images. a representation of something that a human or animal sees.

Visual receptor. a nerve ending that receives visual stimuli.

Vital organs. the inner parts of the body that are necessary in order to sustain life.

Vocal fold. folds of tissue in the throats of some animals that are used to make sound, like a cat's purr.

Vocalization. to produce a sound with the voice.

Vomeronasal organ. the organ snakes and some other animals use to smell.

Warm blooded. an animal that can keep its body warm, regardless of the surrounding temperature.

Waterproof. something that can keep water out.

Whisker. one of the stiff long hairs growing near the nose or mouth of an animal.

Wild. living an undomesticated lifestyle.

Zoologist. a scientist who studies the biology of animals.

Metric Conversions

To convert degrees Fahrenheit to degrees Celsius, subtract 32 and then multiply by .56.
To convert inches to centimeters, multiply by 2.5.
To convert ounces to grams, multiply by 28.
To convert teaspoons to milliliters, multiply by 5.
To convert tablespoons to milliliters, multiply by 15.
To convert fluid ounces to milliliters, multiply by 30.
To convert cups to liters, multiply by .24.

Index